The Spirit of Swimming

Copyright Paula Timpson

2017

For Water Babies everywhere

Adopt the pace of nature

Her secret is patience

Emerson

Blue Is

Blue is pure

Color of calm

Serenity

Freedom

Life

Love

Hope and transfiguration

Inside pools water spins electric blue tales of wisdom

Alaskas ice is so white its blue

The moon too

Reflecting in water leading us

To grace

Flowers

Swimming in blue pools

Is soft as flowers

Blue radiant petals

Water touches

Love

Hope

Salvation

Blue Light

Swimming in the blue light

Is freedom

Found

Alleluia

Swimming is gift

Opening hearts floating gazing up to heaven

From where our help comes from

Blue Breath

Breathe in

Blue light

Swim

Alive

In the mystery

That is

You

Free as

Bluebirds wings

Sing

Swim

Life

Mermaid

A mermaid

Is grace

Openness of heart

Free

Flowing

Blue swirl

Green light

Yellow soul

Arising daily

To

Thank God

For her blessings

In the water

Is pure silence

Magical embrace

Heals

Feel Mermaid

As you swim

See her glow

Follow

Open Hearts

Swimming will

Open hearts

Always

In the joy

Water touches

Grace

Lifts spirits

As birds

Create song

Wont be long until you are

Ready and able to pray and see

The good all around you

Water teaches us

To be

Who we are

Unafraid

Children

Of

God

Pregnant

Pregnant

Tummy full of coconut

And beautiful baby boy

Floating inside

Belly up toward the stars

Hearts alive

Beating as one

Swimming

Pregnant

Awakened

To Gods miracles

Pray

Pray

As you swim

Dreams begin

They happen

In Gods time

When we least expect

Pray and find joy

As you swim

Water tickles hearts

Alive and dancing

Wet with

Anticipation

And waiting

Blue Eyes

The water

Matches his eyes

Our son whose eyes

Transform us all

Into

Hope

Blue shiny sparkling kaleidoscopes of light

Jimmys eyes dance

As he swims and breathes love as he sees

With

Wisdom

Beyond his years

Giving me peace

Swim and Trust

Swim and trust

Pray don't worry

Swims open up

Life

Hope

Baptism

Walk on water

Believe

Arms wingspan is wide

As the sun

Life has just begun

In the Water

In the water

Circles of light

Embrace your heart

Feel

Breathe

Feel wisdom

Deep within your soul

Swimming

Soft petals

Strong energy

Be One

Moving toward freedom

In the water

Wedding Morning

On my wedding day

I woke early

And ran over to the lake to swim

Feeling my inner glow

Praying

Believing

Heart dancing

Living free

Within

God

Filled

Me

Fully

As I

Was ready

To say

I do

Forever

Sounds of Water

Listen into the

Sounds of water

Everywhere

Rain Fish tanks

Waterfalls

The sea

Ponds

Pools

Laughter bubbling free

The Mill River in Fairfield Ct was a

Place we put our feet in the water

Shared pizza and dreamt of what we have now

Magical

For Jimmy

When Jimmy was three we

Swam to the

Magical blue together at

Caspersen sea

Mum and Jimmy are

Forever one

Creating

Swimming

Since conception

Day of birthing I swam

Graceful weightless

Belly up floating

Shining

Happy

Free

Blessed

Forever

Seahorse

We believe in

Seahorse

Sharing

Wrapping tails

Dancing light

Two as one

Forever

Seahorse love is incredibly

Opening and amazing

Surfers

Surfers wait

For just the right moment

To swim

Into the wave

Reaching it balancing standing on surfboard

There is a rhythm

Inside the circle of blue water

Is shiny love

Waving its light

Hopeful in the early morning

Sunrise colors

Just for surfers

Portuguese

There was a little cat

Named Portuguese

Who swam and loved the sea

Little tiny whitecaps rushed in

As Jimmy and I ran playing as children

At the beach as

Portuguese little white cat

Ran into the sea and played too

Healing cat

Freeing cat

Of wonder

Forever in our hearts

Aflame with

Peace

Dolphins

Swimming with the dolphins

Filled me with light

Soon after I became pregnant

With our son

True gift

Heritage from the Lord

Whales Tails

Whales tails are

Magical

Looking like

Peace signs

Rising up out of the sea

Suddenly they appear

Big as life

Listen in to whales breaths

Hearts full of

Sparkling

Morning sunrise

And evening sunset

Colors of heaven

Christh

Christ

Olympic U.S. Divers

Steele Johnson and David Boudia

Praise God

Our identity is Christ

They say

Twirling divers

Inner strength is from God

Trusting they

Win Silver medal

And

Shine

Full of

Gods glory

Philippians 4:6 Do not be anxious about

Anything but in every situation by prayer and petition

With thanksgiving present your requests to God

Wink

Wink

Our

Turkish Van

Enjoyed

The water

In our pool he brought us joy

Swimming

Strong cat

White fur wet sparkled rainbows

Touched grace

Wink healed me

And made me free

When I swim I think of Wink

I feel his love

Keeping me hopeful

And happy

And full of

Rainbows

East Hampton Pool

Big clear cool pool

Full of

Waterfalls and magic

Refreshing as a mountain lake

East Hampton pool

Opened us up to the wisdom within

As we swam and found

Happiness

In simplicity and light

Love is alive in Peace

East Hampton pool

Forever

Memories

Acapulco Pool

We were the only ones there

Ready to share

Best friends in love

Acapulco Pool

Waterfalls and warm embraces

Fun and laughter

Silence and massage

Romance

Acapulco pool

Is a memory of pure love

Morning passion full

Colorful fruits breakfast

Easy free days we shared in

Mexico

Sasco Beach

Mom and I lay on yellow floats

Happy at Sasco Beach in Fairfield Ct

Peaceful seagulls

Drifting on dreams

Jimmy his mom and I swam at the beach

Annadel called me a Dolphin

Enjoying

Grilled cheese sandwiches with tomato

His moms favorite

I love them too

Simple

Pure

Summer joys

Remembered forever

Sherwood Island

We swam and

Ate pizza

At

Sherwood Island

Special beach of

Culture and shade

Friendships that last forever

We covered all the Ct beaches

From one end to the next

Hammonasset and Milford

Pleasure Beach in the old days dad said was beautiful

Shiny silver

We all love to swim

In waters that hold us close

Let us go

Touch us and move us to peace

Our First Date

Sailing we

Capsized on

Our first windy September date

I was happy

Swimming

Being with you

I love to fly and dance

In the water

Be me

Connected

Balanced

Beautiful

By your side

In the wind

On the Catamaran sailboat

Our first date

Remembered

Forever

Oceans Breath

We are all

One

In oceans breath

Winds Angels lift spirits up to heaven

Swimming inside salty sea

Joy radiates

Off waves crashing

Spinning

Grace

Forever

Filling

Our hearts with

Love

Koi Ponds

Koi ponds

Run free in Spring

Bright color big Koi fish swim

And smile

As we feed them at ponds

We have known

All around

Peace

Listening in to the

Water we hear whispers of grace

Leading us to forever

Joy

Twin Brooks Lake

I liked walking out into the

Water at

Twin Brooks Lake

As a young girl

In Ct

Learning to swim with

Graceful strokes and breaths

A rhythm a meditation

Over the years

Swimming

Into a woman

With child

Swimming has been

A true gift

Given from above

A place of peace

And joy

Forever

Stony Brook Home Pool

When I was pregnant

What a blessing it was

To have

Our

Stony Brook home pool

In the Winter inside

Warm soothing water

Baby James felt

A great sense of love

Breathing

In Mums womb

Swimming daily

Dreaming

Praying

So many prayers lived in that pool

Full of hope and trust

Baby James swam the butterfly

He felt true freedom

As a baby in the pool

Marco Polo

Blind we see

By heart and love

Touching our family

Fun laughter

Swimming to capture and discover

Marco Polo

In our pool surrounded by pineapples

The Virgin Mary basil rosemary oranges and lemons

At home

In another world

For awhile

Smiling we

Touch water

And each other

Free

Truly happy

Waves

For Jimmy

You rode the waves as a child

And tell me to listen to them

In Acapulco

Waves are free

Curling embracing your soul

And my heart

As a boy you rode the ocean waves

You believe in and feel the water

In your Spirit forever too

Amazing Grace

Dogs swim

Instantly

When put into the water

Paws pumping

Eyes smiling

Trusting

A baby floats and laughs

Believes in the water holding him up

Amazing grace

We are born trusting

Float

As a hand holds the lower back

And one lets go in trust

Float

Find freedom

Heart sings reaches

Peace

On the water

Salt holds one up

All water supports the body

As if in the womb

A child

Believing

Spirit

Dancing

With the sun

Sunshare

A small simple

Sailboat

We named

Sunshare

Lives forever in our hearts

Wavy wild day we sailed and swam

You guided

With God and your dads

Spirit from heaven the boat

To Fairfields beach home

I felt safe with you

Love was alive

Wave

Launch into every wave Thoreau said

Yes reach out arms wide

Open as if a bird ready to fly

Glide on the water

Weightless free

Hopeful open as a child

Trusting

The water will hold you up

Even when you let go

Breathe

Its all before you now

The long shiny stretch of endless sea

All is up to you and God

Accept life and do what you can

With the rest

Remembering sprinklers and running through

Touching water is

Touching truth

Remarkably solid it is strong as

We are

When we let our bodies and souls

Swim

Writing and Swimming

Writing and swimming are twins

Ideas enter into

Pure openness as wind

Swimming

Souls we have known and loved

Ashes are tossed out to sea

Blending into life anew

Rich shiny waves curl and fold in on the past

Opening the future

To

Anything is possible

Be spontaneous as the sea

As rhythmic as the seasons

And as wild as the wind

Swimming

In silence

Smiling

Younger Days and Now

Whenever I go in to the sea with anyone I love

I feel so happy

Untouchable

Vast expanse of blue turquoise green light

Enriches us bringing peace

Joy and laughter

Talk of dreams and life

Escapes inside salt air and winds

Like kites our lives are carried

And memories too

Senses are opened

As wide as the sea sun and moon

Stars we are

 Shiny nourished by nature

Dog Beach

Dogs love

Dog beach

We all do too

Racing in the wind

Salt water holds dogs up to fly

Goldens and Labs enjoy retrieving

In the sea

Listening to laughter

Feeling their energy and light

Deep inside the water

Swim dogs

We find strength in their eyes

Breathing joy

Assumption Day August 15

Assumption Day

Is the annual

Tradition to

Touch water

Make a wish

I remember

Swimming in Sag Harbor

Long Island

At Long Beach

Praying for a child

Someday

Trusting

Believing

Listening to the salty sea

Speak to me

Signs

I swam at the North Fork beach

On Long Island

Three swans swam with me

A sign

I knew I was pregnant

Deep inside

Signs

Are truth

And

Peace

Gifts of nature

Forever

Full Moon Swims

Full moon swims

Are

Magical

Under

Full moon lights

Love

Our eyes

Gazing

Hearts

Blazing

Peace inside

Us

For

With

God anything is possible

Dreaming of miracles

Charlotte Harbor Freedom Swim

For Andre

Every 4th of July Andre

Swims the Charlotte Harbor Freedom swim

In Punta Gorda

Across the Peace River.

Andres family is there with him

Guiding lights

The sun leads them home

In the sparkling water

Life is beautiful

Eyes are shiny full of hope

Blessed by the music

Birds sing

To our souls

Touching

Leading

All to glory

Bethsaida

There is a pool

In Jerusalem

By the Sheepgate

Called

Bethsaida

Sick people

The blind

Lame

Those with shriveled limbs

Wait

For the

Moving of the water

An Angel would come

Into the pool at certain times

The water was troubled

The first to go into the pool

After it was troubled

Was cured of

Whatever

Infirmity he had

Psalm 37

Delight yourself in the Lord

He will give you the desires of your heart

Pray when you swim

All opens up

To something better

The best is alive

In the water

Speaking to

Your Spirit

Water Is

Water is a powerful force

Of love

Holding you up to the light

Blue waves

Shiny hope

Is ever alive

Gift is water

From our lord

He knows what we need

To survive

And be free

Water is life

Fidget Spinners

Jimmys blue

Fidget spinner

Spins

Like water

Swirls of white and blue

Waves

A blue Angel meditation

It is quiet

Joy

Boys are right

Fidget Spinners are addicting

because

Water silence and laughter are

Peace

Wings

As I swim

I gaze up

From where my help comes from

I see a bird with wide big wings

Flying free

Unexpectedly I find my heart opening

And trusting

Connecting

Parallel with the bird

I am wide winged free and happy

Too

Simple is life

When we relax into its possibilities and trust

As a bird can fly only by believing

So may we

Become hope

Truly seeing

Neptune

Swimming with Neptune

Is pure joy

In the water cream color beautiful Neptune

Is King of the sea

He is truly meant to be

Blonde eyelashes and dark eyes and nose

Pure love

Is Neptune

Natural swimmer

Golden Pyrenees

He is a young active

Boy

Forever alive

Free

Puppy

Harry Potter

Harry Potter

Can swim

Underwater

For an hour

Amazing grace

Breath of light

Of love

Hope and surrender to

The mystery

That is

Life

Lived in freedom

Of creativity

Swimmer Cat

Wink our white cat

Swam in our pool

White fur shined rainbows

A cat free

Shiny in the sun

Unique Wink

Same as our son

Full of surprise and mystery

Laughter and love

Joy in water

Is

Forever

Dogs Love

Dogs swim

And we

Forget everything

Dogs smiles are

Dolphins

Happy

In the moment

As children are

Everyday

Dogs swim and we

Reflect

Their happiness

We are rich

Dogs love

With all they have teaching us

How to give

And live

Sea Green Eyes

I was

Born with

Sea green eyes

Bedroom eyes

My grandma called them

Alive

Burning with light

Passion

Truth

My Dad Grandma and Great Grandpa

Share sea green eyes

The sea lives inside my heart

And eyes

Forever

Sea Foam

Sea foam is

Lemon Meringue pie

Whipped cream

White Lilies blooming

Kites and swans

Gulls swim in sea foam pillows

Floating

In the wind

Sea foam

Sticks to everything

Gifting us with life and love

Sea Foam disappears and we do too

In Gods time

Unforgettable

Energy

Hop e

Renewed

Swim Inside

Swim inside

A painting

Creating

Colors of joy

A blessing it is

To swim

It is

Always possible

With Gods love

One Legged Swimmer

He has one leg

Yet he swims

Beautifully

The magic of swimming

Is anyone can do it

If they believe

And trust the water

I watch him swim

Because he

Inspires my heart

I know

 Any time I want

I can swim

If I am pregnant

If I have one leg

Or no legs

He reaches the end and turns

Swimmers turn

One leg flips up and there he goes

Swimming

You Can Meet

You can meet

People swimming

It is a happy free time

Child like joy

Glows from within

Sunshine and winds fill us up

Lifting spirits high

Naturally

Together in the sea

Or alone

Each is with God

The Spirit of swimming is

Forever alive

Touch water

Breathe love

Grandpa

Grandpa always loved

The sea swimming and fishing

When Grandpa was sick

He wished to go to the water

And put his feet into the salty refreshing sea

I swam crying tears mixing in with waves

Grandpa sat in his wheelchair with

Puffy wheels at the edge of the water

Smiling

Watching me swimming

Free

Free Swimming

Free swimming

Tossing old house keys into the sea

We move on

Grow and

Find

New homes in our hearts

Once swimming

I lost my wedding band and it was gone

Free swimming

My husband gave me a new one same as ever

Because it was gift of

Love

Freedom in the sea

Free swimming

Finding

Being

Believing

Acapulco Pool

Romance

Burned

Deeply in our best friend hearts

In Acapulco pool

Silently swimming

Laughter was alive

Joy immense in the freedom

Of the water

Wind

Touching

Opening hearts

Every morning breakfast

Fresh fruits on colorful Mexican plates

Papaya pineapple mango melons bananas

We smile we share

We are

In to the timelessness

That is us

Gold richness of our love

Is

Best friends forever

Virgin Mary

Blue and white

Is light

The Virgin Mary

Has lived

Near our pools

In the day

In the moonlit nights

Saving us

From ourselves

Sky blue white clouds

Dance dream discover

Hearts form in the warm wind

Of swimming

Opening

Into pure grace of today

Swims With You

We stroke the water

In rhythm

Of us

Shine of eyes

Sparkle of life

Touches our hearts

We are children

In the light

All is right

In the moments

We swim together

Water splashing

Arms reaching

Legs pumping

Breath as one

Our son

Leads us

Home

Gods gift

Butterfly

Swim the Butterfly

Watch them fly

Wings out wide as Florida sunshine

Citrus scents the lanai

Follow your heart

Forever

Swimming

Butterfly

Flying free

Confident

Trusting in

Gods plans

For your

Life

Open wings

Close

Breathe in

Taste rainbow

Warm Mineral Springs

Our son Jimmy first

Went underwater at

The Warm Mineral Springs in

Northport Florida

Mom and I soaked in warm

Mineral waters smiling laughing

Free and happy

Once Jimmy went underwater he loved it

Full of courage

Laughing he kept

Going under

Again and again

His way

Once he likes something he does it

Same as Mum

Over and over

Pure joy

Becomes a meditation

In life

A rhythm of

Hope

And

Happiness

Convent

In Darien Ct

There is a special convent

Called St Birgitta

Once I was there

Walking around and

Saw water

I was led to its wonder

I saw a black and white Nuns habit on the grass

Inside swimming was a nun

So free

Quietly she gazed at the sky

I knew she was

Talking with God

I let her be and

I was free

Knowing

I too do the same as she

Sea Turtles

Sea turtles

Breathe

Life

Fluttering big beautiful

Wings flying under the sea

Silently

They

Gift us with

Joy

And Possibility

Manatee

See Manatee

They appear as

Mermaids

Silent

Floating

Eating lettuce

Sea Cows

Are manatee

Grey and inviting

Holding breaths

A long time under water

Wish we could too

Then we would

Truly

Hear the silence

The truth

Feel the sea world

Living inside the sea

Free

Real beauty

Titanic

They

Listened to the music as the

Ship sank

Swim to freedom

Water is there for us

It is glory

Water of heaven

Is alive

Forever

Water reflects sky

Angels live inside

The Titanic went down

Yet we shall always

Rise

Lifted up

By

Shiny miracle

Of

Water

Starfish

Be a

Starfish

Float

Arms extended

Legs too

Eyes closed

Open see sky clouds moving

Breath touching soul

Spirits rise and let go

As clouds take away all that we

Want to leave

And fill us with

Whatever we need to succeed

Here

Virgin Marys Love

Swim inside

The Virgin Marys love

Shes with you

Gifting you

To believe

Warm is her

Luminous love

In the mystery

Pray

Play

Relive Jesus first miracle

Changing water to wine

Swim inside

The Virgin Marys love

Printed in Great Britain
by Amazon